Walk with Y'shua Through the Jewish Year

Janie-sue Wertheim and Kathy Shapiro

Published by

Purple Pomegranate Productions
San Francisco, California

ACKNOWLEDGMENTS

I am grateful to God for my husband Mark's support throughout this project.   His willingness to do above and beyond at home gave me the gift of time so necessary to fulfill this dream. I am more thankful for him than words can tell!

I am also thankful for the good attitude of my daughters Sarah, Michaela and Hannah. It blesses me to see you walking with Y'shua. My friend Nina Engen was a special support and help, sharing ideas and her gift of threading words together. A special thanks to Collette Hoeschen and Carole Becker who gave quality care to my girls.

—Kathy Shapiro

I want to express my gratitude to David Brickner for letting us run with this idea. Thanks for believing in what we wanted to do, David! I appreciate Ruth Rosen for her friendship and skilled editing. Paige Saunders, our art director, made working on art treatments a delight.

Most of all, I am grateful to God for my husband Steve who pushed me along and frequently ordered take-out so that I could write instead of cook! I am also thankful for my children Ben and Rebekah who prayed along with me every step of the way. This book is really their project as much as it is mine.

—Janie-sue Wertheim

Purple Pomegranate Productions

©1998 by Purple Pomegranate Productions. All rights reserved.
Printed in the United States of America
03 02 01 00   6 5 4 3

ISBN 1-881022-40-4

Art direction
        Paige Saunders
Cover design and illustrations
        Carol Clemons
Design and layout
        Harry J. Johnson

Cataloging in publication data are available through
the Library of Congress.

Wertheim, Janie-sue and
Shapiro, Kathy
        Walk With Y'shua Through the New Year

CONTENTS

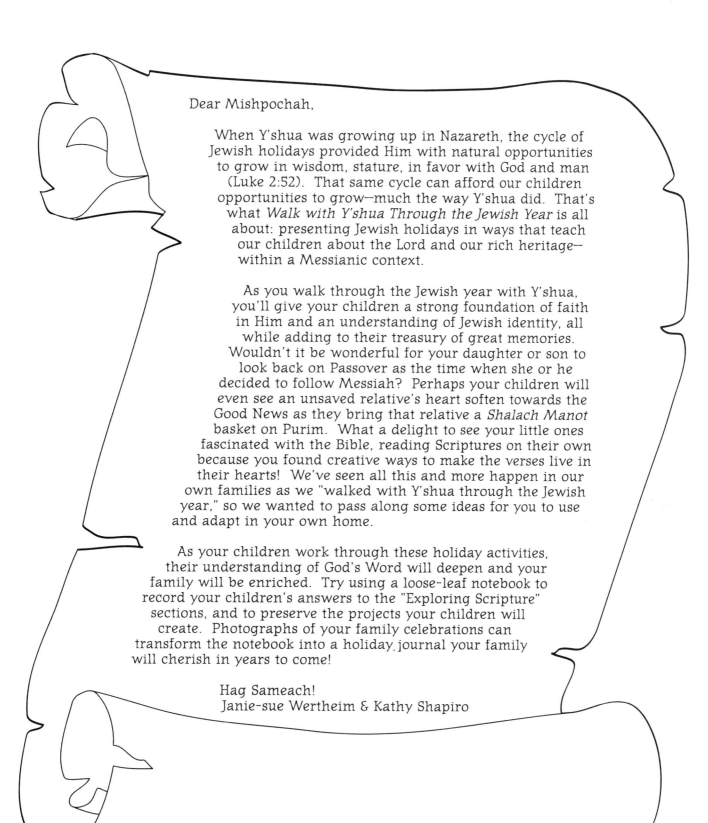

Dear Mishpochah,

When Y'shua was growing up in Nazareth, the cycle of Jewish holidays provided Him with natural opportunities to grow in wisdom, stature, in favor with God and man (Luke 2:52). That same cycle can afford our children opportunities to grow—much the way Y'shua did. That's what *Walk with Y'shua Through the Jewish Year* is all about: presenting Jewish holidays in ways that teach our children about the Lord and our rich heritage—within a Messianic context.

As you walk through the Jewish year with Y'shua, you'll give your children a strong foundation of faith in Him and an understanding of Jewish identity, all while adding to their treasury of great memories. Wouldn't it be wonderful for your daughter or son to look back on Passover as the time when she or he decided to follow Messiah? Perhaps your children will even see an unsaved relative's heart soften towards the Good News as they bring that relative a *Shalach Manot* basket on Purim. What a delight to see your little ones fascinated with the Bible, reading Scriptures on their own because you found creative ways to make the verses live in their hearts! We've seen all this and more happen in our own families as we "walked with Y'shua through the Jewish year," so we wanted to pass along some ideas for you to use and adapt in your own home.

As your children work through these holiday activities, their understanding of God's Word will deepen and your family will be enriched. Try using a loose-leaf notebook to record your children's answers to the "Exploring Scripture" sections, and to preserve the projects your children will create. Photographs of your family celebrations can transform the notebook into a holiday journal your family will cherish in years to come!

Hag Sameach!
Janie-sue Wertheim & Kathy Shapiro

SHABBAT

A BIT OF BACKGROUND

Shabbat is the first holiday God ever created!   After He finished making the world, He made a special day of rest. We read about it in Genesis, the book at the very beginning of the Bible:

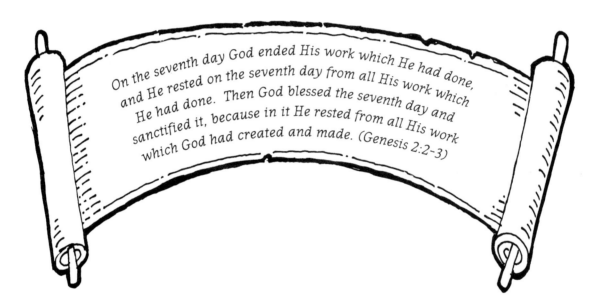

On the seventh day God ended His work which He had done, and He rested on the seventh day from all His work which He had done. Then God blessed the seventh day and sanctified it, because in it He rested from all His work which God had created and made. (Genesis 2:2-3)

God blessed Shabbat and made it special and holy right from the start of creation! If God doesn't get tired like people do, why did He rest? Because He knew that after you work hard and do something good, it's right to stop and enjoy it. God saw that He had done a very good job in creating the world, and so He stopped to appreciate His own work. Later, He taught people how to do the same thing.

DIGGING DEEPER

God gave us Shabbat as a gift to help us rest and find His peace. When Y'shua (Jesus) was on the earth, some people got angry at Him because He healed people on Shabbat. Y'shua made sure people understood that God made Shabbat for people and not the other way around! And when we know Y'shua, every day of the week can be Shabbat in our hearts. Even if we have to go to school and do homework or chores, we can have peace inside because of Y'shua. But if we also set aside the one specific day of the week for Shabbat, we won't be distracted by our everyday routine, so we can stop and enjoy thinking about the good things that we did during the week. Even more important, we can think about all the good things that God has done for us. And we can take this special time to think about Y'shua's love for us. It gives us a peaceful, happy feeling—a small picture of what heaven will be like!

EXPLORING SCRIPTURE

The Jewish people meet Shabbat!

Read: Exodus 16

1. How much manna were the people supposed to collect on ordinary days? What happened if they collected too much?

2. How much manna did God want our people to collect on the sixth day? Did they do it? Did God send manna on the seventh day?

3. What did God want the Israelites to do on the seventh day? Did they do it?

Now read: Matthew 11:28

1. What did Y'shua promise to people who are tired?

2. What did people have to do in order to get what Y'shua promised?

3. What happens to you when you don't get rest?

OUR TRADITIONS

Our Jewish people have symbols that help us say "hello" to Shabbat.
Shabbat begins when the sun goes down on Friday night, and we prepare for it by lighting candles just before sundown. The flames remind us of God's presence, and

that He wants us to live as people of the light. We also recite a special *kiddush* prayer over the fruit of the vine, using a cup that is only for Shabbat and other important events. We eat a special kind of bread called *challah*, but first we say a special blessing for that too. Parents usually say a special blessing for their children

on Shabbat. They ask God to help their children grow in their love for Him.
These are some of the traditional blessings to welcome Shabbat:

The blessing over the Shabbat candles:

בָּרוּךְ אַתָּה יְיָ אֱלֹהֵינוּ מֶלֶךְ הָעוֹלָם אֲשֶׁר קִדְּשָׁנוּ בְּיֵשׁוּעַ הַמָּשִׁיחַ אוֹר הָעוֹלָם.

Baruch atah Adonai, Elohenu Melech ha olam, asher kidshanu b'Y'shua ha Mashiach, or ha olam.
Blessed are You, O Lord Our God, King of the Universe, who has made us holy in
Y'shua the Messiah, the Light of the World.

The blessing over the Kiddush cup:

בָּרוּךְ אַתָּה יְיָ אֱלֹהֵינוּ מֶלֶךְ הָעוֹלָם בּוֹרֵא פְּרִי הַגָּפֶן.

Baruch atah Adonai, Elohenu Melech ha olam, borei, pr'i ha gaffen.
Blessed art Thou, O Lord our God, King of the universe who created the fruit of
the vine.

The blessing over the Challah (special bread):

בָּרוּךְ אַתָּה יְיָ אֱלֹהֵינוּ מֶלֶךְ הָעוֹלָם הַמּוֹצִיא לֶחֶם מִן הָאָרֶץ.

Baruch atah Adonai, Elohenu Melech ha olam, ha motzi lechem min ha aretz.
Blessed art Thou, O Lord our God, King of the Universe who brings forth bread from
the earth.

We also have symbols that help us say "goodbye" to Shabbat and "hello" to the new week.
Shabbat ends on Saturday night as soon as we can see at least three stars in the sky.
We are sad to see Shabbat go, but we are eager to begin the new week serving the

Lord! We say another blessing with the kiddush cup and we smell fragrant spices to
help us remember the sweetness of Shabbat. We light the *Havdalah* candle and watch
it glow for a few moments. Havdalah means "separate" and it reminds us that Shabbat
is set apart from the rest of the week. Now that we've said "good-bye" to Shabbat, we
put out the flame in a bit of wine from the cup . . . and begin our new week with joy.

CELEBRATION IDEAS

• **Make your own Challah**

- 1 cake or package of rapid rise yeast

- 2 teaspoons sugar

- 4 1/2 to 5 cups unbleached white flour

- 1/4 cup warm water (about 3/4 cups more water for step 3)

- 2 teaspoons salt

- 3 eggs

- 2 tablespoons salad oil

- 4 tablespoons sesame or poppy seeds

1. In a small bowl combine 1/4 cup warm water, sugar and yeast. Cover and set aside for 5 minutes.

2. In a very large bowl, put the flour and salt. Make a well and add the oil. Break in 2 of the eggs.

3. In a 1 cup measure, break the egg and put the egg white in it. (refrigerate the yolk for later). Add enough warm water to equal 1 cup.

4. Pour yeast mixture into flour mixture. Mix and add water mixture. Let it rest for 5 minutes.

5. Mix until a dough is formed. Knead 10 minutes or until smooth in elastic. Let raise in a warm place until doubled in bulk (put it in a greased bowl and cover with a clean towel).

6. Punch down, knead a few more minutes and let raise again.

7. Shape into a challah. Glaze with beaten egg yolk and sprinkle on the seeds. Let rise until doubled in bulk. Bake at 375 degrees oven 50-60 minutes until browned.

• **Create a family Shabbat plan**

Record your plan by answering these questions in your journal and drawing pictures to illustrate where possible.

1. What should my family think about as we celebrate Shabbat? What feelings should Shabbat bring to us?
2. How can we make Shabbat different from the rest of our week?
3. What can we do to help us grow close to Y'shua?

• Make a family Tzedakah box

Tzedakah is Hebrew for "righteousness." God wants us to share with those in need. Many Jewish people put Tzedakah boxes in their homes so they can set aside money to help others. If you receive an allowance, you might consider putting some of it into your family's Tzedakah box each Shabbat. You and your family can decide who will receive the money when your Tzedakah box is full.

What you need:

- small can with plastic lid
- Bible verses on giving
- construction paper and/or magazine pictures
- markers
- clear contact paper
- paste

What you do:

Decorate your can by pasting on construction paper, cutouts from magazines, stickers or anything you want. With your marker, add a Bible verse.
Cover your decorated can with clear contact paper.
Cut a hole in the lid for coins.
Use it each Shabbat!

• Make a special family *Siddur* (prayer book):

Use special paper to make a family Siddur.
Make a special cardboard cover and decorate it with pictures of God's creation.
Use a three-hole punch for cover and pages and tie together with ribbon.

Ideas:

- Illustrate the prayers and blessings you put in your Siddur with pictures from calendars and magazines.
- Write out the traditional Shabbat blessings.
- Add other prayers you find in the Bible.
- Put your family Shabbat plan in the Siddur.

A VERSE TO MEMORIZE FOR SHABBAT

Exodus 20:8 "Remember the Sabbath day by keeping it holy."

COLOR YOUR OWN HOLIDAY PICTURE

ROSH HODESH
FESTIVAL OF THE NEW MOON

A BIT OF BACKGROUND

God gave directions in the Torah telling us how to divide up the year according to the months and seasons and celebrations. Regular calendars divide the year into monthly sections according to how long it takes the earth to circle around the sun. The Jewish calendar is special because it divides the year into different monthly sections based on how long it takes the moon to circle around the sun.

Have you ever noticed the different shapes of the moon? We watch the moon go through different stages, and during one of its stages, we can't see it at all! But the first night that it reappears as a slender crescent in the sky it's called a "new moon." And whenever you see that new moon, it's the beginning of a new month on the Jewish calendar.

In ancient times, the festival of the new moon was a major holiday for our people. The shofar was sounded and the people recited special Psalms. The new month was announced from place to place by waving flaming torches on high hills!

DIGGING DEEPER

Rosh Hodesh is a new beginning each month, like a mini-Rosh Hashanah! Our people celebrated God's faithfulness, and this time of renewal of the moon was a time of special rededication to Him. We can use this time to renew our hearts as well, by dedicating the days God has given us in the new month to His service.

EXPLORING SCRIPTURE

Read: Psalm 118:19-26 (This is one of the special Hallel Psalms.)
1. What gates does the Psalm writer want opened?
2. What did God do that makes the Psalm writer want to praise Him?
3. How important was the stone that the builders rejected? What did it become?

Now Read: Acts 3:1-8 and Acts 4:5-12

1. The lame man at the gate of the Temple was hoping to receive money; what did he receive instead?
2. Some of the leaders were upset about what Peter did for the lame man. What did they ask him?
3. When Peter answered their question, he told them about Y'shua and quoted a verse from the Psalm we just read. Go back to the Psalm and see which verse he quoted. How is Y'shua like the stone?
4. Is there salvation in any other besides Y'shua? Have you accepted His salvation?

OUR TRADITIONS

The special Psalms recited on Rosh Hodesh are called *Hallel* Psalms. Hallel comes from the Hebrew word, "hallelujah" which means "praise the Lord!" These Psalms praise God for who He is in His faithfulness, mercy, and love.

God is the Great King —PSALM 113

- Psalm 113—God is the Great King
- Psalm 114—God delivered His people from Egypt with power
- Psalm 115 —God keeps His promises
- Psalm 116—God delivered my soul from death
- Psalm 117—Everybody, Praise the Lord!
- Psalm 118—God's mercy endures forever

Today in the synagogue, Jewish people say special prayers for the beginning of the new moon but the holiday is not as festive as it used to be in Bible times.

CELEBRATION IDEAS

• Rosh Hodesh Picnic

What you need:

Plan a late-evening picnic with your parents when the new moon is supposed to appear.

- blanket
- favorite treats to enjoy
- Bible
- Jewish calendar

What you do:

Look on your Jewish calendar to find out when to celebrate Rosh Hodesh.

Plan a late-evening picnic.

Go to a picnic spot.

Find the new moon!

Read Psalm 118, either taking turns or altogether. As you read, remember who gives us salvation.

Bless and praise God saying, "Blessed are you, Adonai our God, who has told the moon to renew itself."

Enjoy being together!

A VERSE TO MEMORIZE FOR ROSH HODESH

Psalm 118:22-23 "The stone which the builders rejected has become the chief cornerstone. The LORD has done this, and it is marvelous in our eyes."

COLOR YOUR OWN HOLIDAY PICTURE

ROSH HASHANAH

A BIT OF BACKGROUND

Rosh Hashanah falls in the seventh month of the Jewish calendar, the month called *Tishri*. Just as Shabbat, the seventh day of the week, is set apart from the other days, Tishri, the seventh month is set apart from the other months. Rosh Hashanah, the traditional Jewish New Year, falls during Tishri. It's a happy time when many people buy new clothes and send each other greeting cards—but it is also a serious time.

This holiday is called by many different names. Rosh Hashanah is Hebrew for "the head of the year." But the holiday is also called "the Day of Judgment," because Jewish people who don't yet know Y'shua believe that God opens up the Book of Life on Rosh Hashanah. Then, many people think that on Yom Kippur, He writes His judgments for the coming year for everyone on earth. But Rosh Hashanah has yet another name: *Yom Truah*, which is Hebrew for "The Feast of Trumpets." And that is the name God used for the holiday in the Bible.

In Bible times, God used a musical instrument called a *shofar* (a kind of trumpet made from a ram's horn) to get our attention, to warn us and to help us think about Him. The sound let our ancestors know, "The Lord has something important to say!" For example, in Exodus 19 and 20, God was giving us the Ten Commandments, the rules He wanted us to live by. The loud blasts of the shofar said, "Listen carefully, Israel!" Along with the sound of the shofar there was smoke, fire, thunder, lightning, and the mountain even started to shake!

However, in the New Covenant, we see that the shofar has an even more important announcement to make! The shofar will sound to let the whole world know that Y'shua has returned to bring His people home to heaven, to live with Him forever (1 Thessalonians 4:13-18). All of us who love Y'shua are waiting for that special time!

DIGGING DEEPER

Rosh Hashanah is the beginning of *Yamim Noraim;* that is Hebrew for "the Days of Awe." The Days of Awe call our people to turn to God, which means turning away from sin. It is a time to look deep inside our hearts and pray as King David did: "See if there is any wicked way in me, and lead me in the everlasting way" (Psalm 139:24). This very serious 10-day period lasts until the end of Yom Kippur.

It's a time to think about God and to ask ourselves: "Am I pleasing God by my choices each day? Am I living the way God wants me to?" If you have hurt someone, this is the time to say, "I'm sorry," and to ask forgiveness. Remember that God cares about all people, so when we hurt someone, we've not only wronged a person but we have wronged God. We need to say we're sorry to God as well as to the people we have wronged.

We know that because of Y'shua, God will forgive our sins. But it's still good for us to turn away from sin. And the sound of the shofar on Rosh Hashanah reminds us to do that.

EXPLORING SCRIPTURE

The Akedah, the Binding of Isaac
Read: Genesis 22:1-18

1. When God asked Abraham to make a sacrifice, He asked him to give up the hardest thing in the world. What did he ask Abraham to sacrifice? How did Abraham respond?
2. What did Isaac ask his father? How did Abraham respond?
3. Does the Bible say that Isaac argued or struggled with his father?
4. What did God do when He saw that Abraham was willing to do the hardest thing in the world for Him?
5. Abraham trusted God so much that he knew no matter what God asked him to do, it would turn out OK. Can you think of a time when God wanted you to do something you didn't want to do but you obeyed Him anyway? How did it turn out?

Do you know that Y'shua is God's son? In a way, Y'shua is like the ram in the thicket that you just read about in Genesis. God provided that ram so that Isaac would not have to die. And God provided His own son, Y'shua, to be the sacrifice for our sin so we would not have to die. Unlike Isaac, Y'shua actually experienced death—but God raised Him from the dead!

OUR TRADITIONS

Jewish people still use the shofar to celebrate Rosh Hashanah today. You have to blow awfully hard to play it, but it makes an awesome sound when you do it right. That sound reminds us that God is not far way, but very close to us, involved in our lives. He says through the sound of the shofar: "I love you. Pay attention!"

Some shofars are small. Some are long and curly. Whatever the size or shape, a shofar is sounded three ways:

tekiah   a long clear note
shevarim   three short notes
truah   nine very short notes

The *Tekiah Gedolah* (mighty blast) is the last sounding of the shofar done on Rosh Hashanah. It is a very long, powerful blast.

It is also Jewish tradition to send greeting cards that say *"L'shana tova"* which means "have a good year." And we eat sweet treats on Rosh Hashanah as we ask God to give us a sweet new year.

An interesting and fun tradition called *Tashlich* (which means "to toss away") is based on Micah 7:18-19. In that passage, the prophet says God will forgive us and throw all our sins into the depths of the sea. It is traditional for Jewish people who live near an ocean or a river or a moving stream to go to the water and throw in any crumbs or lint that is stuck deep down in their pockets. This reminds us that God reaches deep down in our souls to clean out our sin.

CELEBRATION IDEAS

• **Adapt the traditional greeting.** We can add something to the greeting: L'shana Tova b' Y'shua ha Mashiach. That means "have a good year in Jesus, the Messiah!"

• **Eat apples dipped in honey.** This traditional holiday goody encourages us to look back on God's faithfulness in the past year, as well as to look forward to the sweet new year God has for us.

15

• **Make a round challah.** Use the same recipe for a Shabbat challah, but instead of braiding the dough, form it into a round loaf. The circular shape of the bread for Rosh Hashanah represents a crown. It reminds us that God is a mighty Ruler, the King of our lives. It also reminds us that we need to make good choices to obey Him in the coming year.

• **Make your own holiday cards** to send to friends and relatives. Before you send them, pray for each friend and relative to grow in his or her relationship with God or to become a believer in Y'shua if they don't already know Him.

• **Have your own Tashlich Family Service**
What you need:
  - walking shoes
  - a bag of bread crumbs
  - a Bible
  - a moving body of water like a river or stream

What you do:
Go with your family to the body of water.
Give each person some of the bread crumbs.
Throw the crumbs into the moving water and watch them float away.
Understand that the crumbs represent our sins, the wrong things we have done. The moving water represents God's forgiveness and mercy flowing toward us.
Read Micah 7:18-19.
Worship by singing your favorite songs about God's love and forgiveness.

A VERSE TO MEMORIZE FOR ROSH HASHANAH
1 John 1:9 "If we confess our sins, He is faithful and just to forgive us our sins and to cleanse us from all unrighteousness."

YOM KIPPUR

A BIT OF BACKGROUND

Rosh Hashanah and Yom Kippur are referred to together as "The High Holidays" or "The High Holy Days." Of the two, Yom Kippur (Hebrew for "Day of Covering") is considered the holiest and most serious day of the year. It is a time to think about our sin. For many Jewish people who don't know Y'shua, it is a day of anxiety. The Bible teaches that our sin separates us from our holy God, so we cannot approach Him without atonement (covering) for our sin. Many Jewish people hope if they do good deeds throughout the year, like giving to charity, God will forgive the bad things they think or do. Then, on Yom Kippur they pray and fast (do without food) and hope that is good enough to satisfy God. Yet many people who do this wonder, "Are my sins really forgiven?" And they are right to wonder, because our Bible tells us a very different story of what atonement is about.

Think of atonement as "at-one-ment," because that's what it means: to make us at one—at peace—with God. God's atonement protected our people just like a blanket, covering the sin that otherwise kept us separated from God.

God gave Moses specific instructions about what to do in order to have our sins covered. The High Priest had to put the blood of the sacrificed animal on the altar. That was God's way of showing us how very serious our sins are. The High Priest had to make those sin-offerings each year. Moses' brother, Aaron, was the first High Priest. He had a very important job. The people waited anxiously as Aaron followed God's special instructions step by step. It was the only day of the year when the High Priest would be allowed into the presence of God in the Holy of Holies. If he tried to come at any other time, he would die! By obeying God's instructions, Israel showed that we wanted Him to rule over us.

DIGGING DEEPER

We no longer have a Temple or a High Priest in Israel. That is why people who don't know God's whole plan wonder if He has really forgiven them when they pray and fast. God loves us and wants to forgive us but if we try to make our own plan to please Him, we will fall short no matter how hard we try! His special plan is the only one that works.

Without a Temple and a High Priest to follow all the special instructions, how can God forgive us? Well, in the New Covenant book of Hebrews, God talks about a different High Priest who made atonement for our sins. This High Priest would make a very different sacrifice—His own life. You see, the blood of an animal could only paint a picture of what God planned to do. That picture had to be painted over and over. But it was always God's plan to provide a perfect covering for our sin. Can you guess who the High Priest is? Y'shua the Messiah is our High Priest—and our sacrifice! When He came to take the punishment for our sins, He accomplished God's whole plan. We don't have to keep painting a picture of what God will do because He already did it!

When Y'shua died, the big thick curtain that led to the Holy of Holies was torn from top to bottom (Luke 23:44-46). God ripped that curtain open to show us that He accepted Y'shua's sacrifice completely—there was nothing to keep people from going into the presence of God in the Holy of Holies! Now we don't have to be afraid to come into God's presence. We can talk to Him from our hearts, and ask for His forgiveness because of what Y'shua, our great High Priest, did for us.

EXPLORING SCRIPTURE

Read: Leviticus 17:11

1. What makes atonement for sin?

2. Who gives us what we need for atonement?

Now read: Hebrews 9:11-15

1. Before Y'shua came, the High Priest had to make sacrifices every year on the day of atonement. How many times did Y'shua have to make a sacrifice?

2. Before Y'shua came, whose blood did the High Priest use? Whose blood did Y'shua use?

3. What gets cleansed, according to verse 14?

4. What do you think is the best part about having Y'shua for our High Priest?

OUR TRADITIONS

The night before Yom Kippur, Jewish people go to the synagogue, for the *Kol Nidre* service. *Kol Nidre* literally means "all vows." It is an ancient prayer that dates back to the Middle Ages, chanted solemnly to a sad melody. In the morning, Jewish people go back to synagogue. Services are held all day. One prayer, the *Al Chet*, lists all the sins our people are asking God to forgive. Everyone is happy when it is time to break the fast at the end of the long day!

CELEBRATION IDEAS

- **Everyone make a list of all the things you can think of that you are sorry for;** things you want God to forgive you for. (You don't have to sign your name on your list.) At the end of the day, each person pastes or tapes his or her list securely to a helium-filled balloon. Take a family walk or drive to a hill or some other special place you agree on and release the balloons with your list of sins. As they disappear from sight, remember that God promises to take our sins far away from us.

- **About fasting:** we don't have to fast for God to forgive us but it can be a good way to remind ourselves of our sin and Y'shua's sacrifice.

- **Plan a special meal to share when the fast is over.** This is a fun way to celebrate God's forgiveness with family and friends.

A VERSE TO MEMORIZE FOR YOM KIPPUR

Psalm 103:12 "As far as the east is from the west, so far has He removed our transgressions from us."

COLOR YOUR OWN HOLIDAY PICTURE

SUKKOT

A BIT OF BACKGROUND

God brought our Jewish people out of Egypt with great miracles, yet we failed to trust Him on the way to the Promised Land. So God had to teach our people how to believe in Him before we entered the Land—and it took 40 years of wandering in the wilderness to do it! During that time, we had no houses to live in; instead we made temporary booths (sukkot) to shelter us. Whenever God moved us on, we'd take down our sukkot, building them again somewhere else. Without the Lord's blessings, we would not have survived all those years in the desert! But He was faithful and supplied all the food, water and protection we needed.

When God finally brought us to "the Land of milk and honey," our ancestors became farmers. God provided rain from heaven to make the crops grow. The olives hung ripe on the trees and the golden wheat stood tall in the fields. Our people had everything they needed, and they lived in nice houses. Still, once a year during harvest time, they built booths and lived in them for one week. God had commanded that this be done so that we would never forget how we lived in booths when He was with us in the wilderness (Leviticus 23: 39-43). He wanted this to be a joyful time, a wonderful holiday. We call it "The Feast of Tabernacles" (another way to say booths) or Sukkot.

Our people looked through the *sukkah* branches at the stars in the sky. They remembered that God provided both rain and harvest as He promised. God's faithfulness brings us joy. No wonder Sukkot is called "The Season of our Joy"—in Hebrew, *Z'man Simhatenu!*

DIGGING DEEPER

When Y'shua was on earth, Jewish families celebrated Sukkot by going up to Jerusalem and bringing many sacrifices to the Temple. And they prayed with all their hearts for rain for the next year's crops. Without rain there would be no harvest and no food.

The last day of Sukkot is called Hoshana Rabah, "The Day of the Great Hosanna." To show our hope for rain for Israel's crops, the High Priest poured water from the pool of Siloam into a basin at the foot of the altar. That water was also a symbol to our people of God's Spirit. Y'shua attended the Temple service on Hoshana Rabah. He spoke to our people, claiming to be the answer to their Sukkot prayers when He said, "If anyone is thirsty, let him come to me and drink!" (John 7:37).

There are different kinds of thirst, not only the need to drink something. We need good friends who know and accept us. We need to feel safe. We need to feel important to the people we love. These needs are like a thirst in our hearts. What other needs do you have? Jesus said we should go to Him when our hearts are thirsty.

In Y'shua's time, our people looked forward to the day when God would pour out His Spirit so they could know Him in a very personal way. Y'shua sent His Spirit to be our helper and comforter. We can have God's presence in our hearts all the time!

EXPLORING SCRIPTURE

Read: Leviticus 23:33-43
1. What did God tell our people to do?
2. What did they use to rejoice before the Lord on Sukkot?
3. What does building a sukkah help us remember?

Now Read: John 7:37-43
1. What did Y'shua invite people to do?
2. Did anyone believe Him? Did everyone believe Him?
3. Y'shua's invitation still holds true today. Does anyone believe Him? Does everyone believe Him? Do you?

OUR TRADITIONS

For Sukkot today, many of our people build booths in their backyards and decorate them with hanging fruit to remember the days when we were farmers in the Land of Israel. In some places, people build a big booth at their congregation instead. During synagogue services we wave a *lulav*, which is made from binding three kinds of branches together. The palm branch is tall and strong, providing support like a person's spine. Willow leaves, shaped like lips, remind us to use our words to praise God and to help others. The eye-shaped myrtle leaves remind us to look at what is right and good. The lemon-like citrus fruit we use is called an *etrog*. Its heartlike shape is to remind us that our hearts belong to God. We wave the *etrog* and *lulav* in all directions, remembering that God is everywhere.

CELEBRATION IDEAS

• **Build a sukkah!** If your family can't make one outside, make one in your bedroom using sheets tied to furniture and silk leaves or construction paper leaves for the roof. Tape glow-in-the-dark stars on the ceiling. Have snacks and devotions in the sukkah. Look up at the stars and have a slumber party in your sukkah.

• **Decorate a sukkah** with fruit to show joy in God's provision for us, and that God decorates our lives with the fruit of the Spirit. Using Galatians 5:22 as a guide, identify the different kinds of spiritual fruit. Use construction paper to cut out fruit shapes and label them with the fruit described in the verse. Use your "spiritual fruit" to help decorate the sukkah. Pray for God to help that fruit grow in your life. Choose a fruit of the Spirit each day during Sukkot. Find ways to show that good fruit to one another.

• **Donate food** to a local food pantry for the poor. This is a way to "give to the Lord according to the blessing He has given you" (Deuteronomy 16:17).

A VERSE TO MEMORIZE FOR SUKKOT

Galatians 5:22 "But the fruit of the Spirit is love, joy, peace, patience, kindness, goodness, faithfulness, gentleness, and self-control."

COLOR YOUR OWN HOLIDAY PICTURE

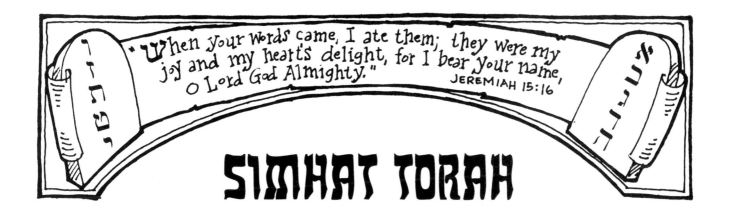

"When your words came, I ate them; they were my joy and my heart's delight, for I bear your name, O Lord God Almighty." JEREMIAH 15:16

SIMHAT TORAH

A BIT OF BACKGROUND

Each Shabbat, Jewish people all over the world read the same weekly portion or *sedrah,* from the Torah, the first five books of the Bible. It takes an entire year to complete the cycle of Torah readings. When this cycle is done, our people celebrate and rejoice over the law—that's what Simhat Torah means. Take a look at your Jewish calendar. The different Scripture readings for each Shabbat are written on it. On Simhat Torah, we read from the last chapter of Deuteronomy and then begin all over again with the first chapter of Genesis.

DIGGING DEEPER

Although Simhat Torah is not a holiday you'll find in the Bible, believers in Y'shua can learn some special things from it. God wants us to truly enjoy studying His Word

Some experiences are so wonderful that you want to do them again and again. Ever see a good movie more than once? Eager to play that new game another time? That is how it is with Simhat Torah, one of the happiest holidays of the Jewish year. It's the day we rejoice in beginning a new season of reading and studying God's Word. As we study the Scriptures, we hear God calling us to a deeper friendship with Him. Just like King David, we want to say from our hearts, "Oh, how I love your law!   I meditate on it all day long!" (Psalm 119:97).

We rejoice in the gift of God's Word because it brings us His message of eternal life. Our Jewish people who don't yet know Y'shua focus on the first five books of the Bible, known as the Law of Moses or the Pentateuch.   But as believers in Messiah, we rejoice over all of God's Word—not just the Torah, but the Prophets, the Writings, and the *Brit Hadashah,* or New Testament. We rejoice over the Law because the Law of Moses clearly points to our Messiah, Y'shua! (John 5:39).

God promised long ago that He would write His law on our hearts and in our minds. Then His law would become more than a bunch of rules to us—God's Spirit would make His Word live in our hearts! (Jeremiah 31:31-34). God kept this promise through Y'shua!

EXPLORING SCRIPTURE

Read: Psalm 119:105

1. What does a lamp or a light do?

2. If you were on a path at night with no light, what would happen?

3. How is God's Word a lamp and a light for you? Can you give three examples of what God's Word helped you to see?

Now Read: John 1:1-4

1. These verses are talking about Y'shua. What is He called in the first verse?
2. Compare these verses to Psalm 119:105. What important word do you see in both places? What do Y'shua and the Bible have in common? What existed first, Y'shua or the Bible?
3. When people are afraid of the dark, they turn on a light. What can you do when you are afraid?

TORAH (THE LAW)   NEVIIM (THE PROPHETS)   KETUVIM (THE WRITINGS)   B'RIT HADASHAH (THE NEW TESTAMENT)

"All scripture is—God breathed and is useful for teaching, rebuking, correcting and training in righteousness, so that the man of God may be thoroughly equipped for every good work."

2.TIM. 3: 16-17

OUR TRADITIONS

Some congregations celebrate Simhat Torah with a special service where young and old take part together. The Torah scrolls are taken out of their special place in the Ark and the adults carry them around the sanctuary. Children follow them like a parade, waving flags, carrying miniature Torah scrolls and dancing with great joy!

CELEBRATION IDEAS

• **Study Psalm 119 with your family.** This Psalm helps us to love God's Word and tells us how the Scriptures guide, instruct, protect and comfort our hearts. Each section of Psalm 119 begins with a letter of the Hebrew alphabet. While you study each section learn or review your Hebrew!

- **Have a Simhat Torah Parade.** Includes special flags for the children to wave. These can be Israeli flags or homemade flags depicting Bible stories or themes. Make your own Simhat Torah flag. Invite special friends to join with you in a Simhat Torah parade. Include a Bible story, singing, dancing and eating!

- **The weekly reading cycle** includes *Haftarah* readings (from the Prophets or Writings), which are meant to be read through during the year. When the rabbis created this schedule, they left out a very important Scripture passage: Isaiah 53. Isaiah 53 tells us how to recognize the Messiah Y'shua. Because our people don't read this section throughout the year, they are missing an important way to find Y'shua. Add this to your calendar reading so your family will know how to recognize Messiah Y'shua. Then you can really rejoice on Simhat Torah!

A VERSE TO MEMORIZE FOR SIMHAT TORAH

Psalm 119:105 "Your word is a lamp to my feet, and a light to my path."

COLOR YOUR OWN HOLIDAY PICTURE

A GREAT MIRACLE
HAPPENED THERE
נס גדול היה שם

HANUKKAH

A BIT OF BACKGROUND

Throughout the history of the Jewish people, wicked people have tried to wipe us out—but God's power has always preserved us. One evil ruler, *Antiochus Epiphanes*, tried to destroy our people by making us serve false gods. A brave Jewish family, the Maccabees, defeated that evil man, but it was God's power that enabled the small band of Israelites to defeat the mighty Greek army.

Tradition says that after the Maccabees cleansed and dedicated the Temple, there was only enough oil for one day. Miraculously, the oil lasted for eight days! That is why the holiday is also called "The Festival of Lights."

DIGGING DEEPER

Hanukkah is such a well-known holiday for Jewish families, yet the only Scripture that mentions Hanukkah is in the New Covenant!

When Y'shua was here on earth, the Roman government ruled over us. Our people longed for freedom. Many thought Messiah would come as a great warrior to defeat the Romans. But God wanted to give His people more than a temporary victory over an earthly ruler. God sent Y'shua to defeat sin and death so that we could love and worship Him.

The worst thing that Antiochus Epiphanes did was try to turn the Jewish people away from God. He put a big idol (false god) and sacrificed a pig in the Temple to keep our people from worshipping the one true God. Sometimes we can get so caught up in thinking of the oil that lasted eight days that we forget the reason for the oil. It was to dedicate the Temple so that we could worship God properly once again. Hanukkah is a fun holiday, but it's also a time to think of ourselves as temples. If you have invited Y'shua into your heart, the Bible says His Holy Spirit lives inside of you just like God's Spirit once dwelled in the Temple. When we allow other people or things to be more important to us than God, it's like having idols in our hearts.

Hannukah is a great time to make sure we are putting God first and that our hearts are nice, clean places for the Holy Spirit to live. We can ask God to cleanse us and help us be rededicated just like the Temple was rededicated. If we do, God will make a miracle in our hearts. Because even if we don't have all the goodness it takes to put God first, God will provide what we need to dedicate ourselves to Him just like He provided the extra oil for the Temple.

EXPLORING SCRIPTURE

Read: John 10:22-28; 40-42

1. Verse 22 is talking about Hanukkah. What other name does the Bible use for the holiday?
2. What did the Jewish leaders ask Y'shua when they saw Him walking in the Temple?
3. What had Y'shua already done to answer their question and why didn't they believe?
4. What do Y'shua's sheep do? What gift does Y'shua give to His sheep?
5. Are you one of Y'shua's sheep? Have you received His gift?
6. What are some ways that you can do what Y'shua says in verse 27?

OUR TRADITIONS

Each night of Hannukah finds Jewish people lighting the hanukkiah (or Hanukkah menorah). We add a candle for each night until the whole menorah is aglow.

Jewish children also play a game with tops called *dreidels* during Hannukah. Some believe that this tradition began when King Antiochus forbade our people to study the Torah. They say these tops were kept handy when students gathered to study the forbidden scrolls. If Greek soldiers appeared unexpectedly, the scrolls were hidden and out came the tops, so it appeared the children had gathered merely to play.

The four sided dreidel with a Hebrew letter on each side tells a story. The letter "nun" stands for *nes* which means miracle. "Gimel" stands for *gadol*, which means great. "Hay" stands for *haya* which means happened.
And "shin" stands for *sham* which means there.
So the message on the dreidel is, "A great miracle happened there!"

Special holiday foods include potato latkes and doughnuts. These treats, which are fried in oil, remind us once again of the miracle of the Temple dedication.

CELEBRATION IDEAS

- **Light your menorah!**

The *shamash* candle is lit first. *Shamash* is Hebrew for "servant," and the servant candle brings light to all the rest. It reminds us of Y'shua, who came as a servant to be the Light of the world.

Place your candles from right to left in your Hanukkiah. Light the shamash candle first. Light your other candles from left to right so that you are lighting the newest day's candle first.

- **Play Dreidel**

What you need:
  - a dreidel and Hanukkah gelt, (coins—real or chocolate)
  - Divide the gelt evenly among players. Everyone puts a piece of gelt in a center pile, or "pot."

What you do:
  - The first person spins the dreidel.
  - The dreidel will land on one of four Hebrew letters and the person who spins acts according to that letter:
  - *nun*=takes nothing from the pot; *hay*=takes half, *gimel*=takes all, (after which each person contributes one piece to the pot); and *shin*=puts one in.
  - Decide how many turns everyone will take spinning the dreidel or how long you will play so no one feels cheated when you stop!

- **Read the story of Hanukkah** (or dress up as Maccabees and act it out) from your favorite holiday book or from 1 Maccabees 4:30-59 in the Apocrypha.

- **Throw a Hanukkah party!** Make and enjoy potato latkes or *sufganyiot* (fried dough-nuts). Play and sing holiday music.

- **Play "Shamash for a day!"** Decorate a shoe box to look like a candle. Each family member writes several ideas for how to serve one another—each idea on a separate slip of paper, (Ideas: pray for Mom and Dad, make someone's bed besides your own, share a special treat, share a Bible verse, etc.). Each day of Hanukkah, family members take turns being the shamash. The shamash's job is to pull out at least one idea and do it the following day. What a way to shine Y'shua's light, by being a servant like Him!

A VERSE TO MEMORIZE FOR HANUKKAH

1 Corinthians 3:16 "Do you not know that you are a temple of God, and that the Spirit of God dwells in you?"

COLOR YOUR OWN HOLIDAY PICTURE

Y'SHUA'S BIRTHDAY

A BIT OF BACKGROUND

Many Jewish people who don't yet know Y'shua find Christmas a bit unsettling. Many of the Christmas carols, greeting cards and decorations are constant reminders to our people of what they don't believe. They certainly would never see Christmas as part of the Jewish calendar. However, for believers in Y'shua, celebrating the birth of our Messiah can be a wonderful and joyful experience. And even if we don't know exactly which day of the year it was, the birth of the Jewish Messiah ought to be part of our calendar celebration. For some families, it wouldn't be Y'shua's birthday without special decorations and lights. Others prefer not to make these things part of the celebration. However your family celebrates, keeping your focus on Y'shua is the most important thing. Whatever you do, celebrate Him!

DIGGING DEEPER

The focus on presents, purchases and decorations makes it possible for people to "celebrate Christmas" without celebrating Y'shua. Even believers can be tempted to get so caught up in gift-giving that we forget God's gift to our Jewish people and the whole world. "For God so loved the world that He gave His one and only Son, that whoever believes in Him shall not perish but have eternal life" (John 3:16). This is the real reason for the season!

EXPLORING SCRIPTURE

The Hebrew prophets told us a great deal about the birth and life of the Messiah so we would be able to recognize Him when He came. It's fun to see how the details of Y'shua's birth in the New Covenant match up with the prophecies of the Hebrew Bible.

Compare the following passages:
1. Isaiah 7:14 and Luke 1:30-35
   What made the Messiah's birth such a special sign from God? How was the Messiah's mother different from any other woman who ever had a baby?

2. **Psalm 89:34-37 and Luke 2:4 & 3:31**

   The Hebrew Scriptures tell how the Messiah would be a descendant of a King of Israel. The New Covenant confirms His royal lineage. What is the name of the king the Messiah came from? How long will the seed, or descendant, of this king rule?

3. **Micah 5:2 and Luke 2:4**

   Where was the Messiah to be born?

4. **Isaiah 9:2, Isaiah 49:6-7 and Luke 2:25-32**

   All of these passages have a word that might remind you of Hanukkah—what is it? (Hint: it begins with the letter "L.") What was the Messiah supposed to do about the darkness? What do you think darkness represents?

OUR TRADITIONS

Unfortunately, there are no Jewish traditions to help us celebrate Y'shua's birthday because the majority of our people believe a mistaken tradition that says He is not our Messiah. Here's a true story of one boy named Jhan who discovered that tradition is not always right.

I was raised in New York City and, like many other Jewish boys, I attended Talmud-Torah (Hebrew school) each day after regular school to study Hebrew, Jewish tradition and history. My father's tailor shop was two blocks away from my Hebrew school. Across the street was one of the biggest churches I had ever seen! I passed it everyday as I walked from Hebrew school to my father's shop.

One December afternoon, I saw something unusual on the front lawn of the church. There were three figures of men with turbans, carrying boxes. There were life-sized toy animals: goats and sheep. There was a small shed with three figures—a mother, a father and a little baby doll in a wooden box of hay. A large sign said, "Born is the King of Israel." I didn't know a lot when I was seven, but I did know that we Jews were Israel and the Gentiles who attended that church were not. My first thought was, "Someone delivered this stuff to the wrong address. It belongs down the street in front of the synagogue!"

I ran to my father's shop as fast as my legs could carry me and yelled, "Daddy,

Daddy! Somebody made a BIG mistake!" My dad told me in a quiet voice that the baby in the manger didn't belong in front of the synagogue. "That king," my father said softly, "is not our king." From that point on, I always wondered about this very strange thing: Why would Gentiles acknowledge the King of Israel while our Jewish people would not?

When I grew up, I came to know Y'shua as my Savior. Then God called me to go and tell our people the good news that our Messiah has come. I still feel sad to think of Jewish boys and girls who don't know that the baby who was born in Bethlehem is the King of Israel. We have wonderful news for them: "Unto you is born this day in the city of David a Savior, who is Messiah the Lord" (Luke 2:11). Y'shua is not only for the Gentiles but for our Jewish people, too!

CELEBRATION IDEAS:

- **Have a birthday party for Y'shua!** Make invitations asking your friends to come celebrate Y'shua's birth. Use this time to share the story of His love. Have a birthday cake for Him and if anyone asks where the "birthday boy" is, explain that He is in your heart. (It's important that the invitations make it clear that the party is about Y'shua, because you might have some friends who are not allowed to come to parties about Him.)

- **Read the story of Y'shua's birth from the Gospel of Luke.** Light a candle to remind you that He came to be the Light of the World. List the ways His coming into the world and into our hearts makes a difference.

- **Give a present to Y'shua!** It might be donating some of your time or money in Y'shua's name to someone needing help. It might be deciding to do your chores without being told, knowing that Y'shua is pleased when we obey our parents. It might be writing Him a poem thanking Him for what He did for you. Whatever present you decide to give, it should make you happy to think how He will enjoy receiving it!

- **Make a holiday wreath with a Jewish touch.** You might use blue and white ribbons. Attach ornaments like a little toy lamb as a reminder that Y'shua is the Lamb of God and a *Mogen David* (Star of David) as a reminder that He is Jewish. If you have room for a small banner on the wreath (or just above it) you can write "Merry Messiahmas" to help visitors understand that Christmas is a celebration of Y'shua, the Jewish Messiah.

A VERSE TO MEMORIZE FOR Y'SHUA'S BIRTHDAY

Luke 2:11 "Today in the town of David a Savior has been born to you; He is Messiah, the Lord."

COLOR YOUR OWN HOLIDAY PICTURE

TU B' SHEVAT

A BIT OF BACKGROUND

The Jewish calendar month of Shevat marks the beginning of spring in Israel even though in the United States we are still in the middle of winter! At this time, the trees in Israel are waking to life again after the long cold season. The word *"tu"* means 15, which is the day that we celebrate this "New Year" for the trees in Israel.

DIGGING DEEPER

As we celebrate on the 15th of Shevat, we remember that God has called us to new life through Y'shua, our Messiah. Think of all the wonderful ways God has used trees (and other growing things) to illustrate His truth and the relationship He wants us to have with Him! For example, in Isaiah 61:3 God says that His people will be called, "trees of righteousness, the planting of the LORD, that He might be glorified."

In Jewish tradition, our Torah is called *Etz Chaim,* the Tree of Life, because Proverbs 3:18 says that God's Word is a tree of life to us. God promised that if we hold on tightly to the wisdom we find in His word, we will be blessed. This idea of staying connected to God's tree of life is very important. Y'shua taught us that He is the vine and we are like branches. To grow strong in our faith, we need to stay close to Him and depend on Him, just as a branch is connected to the vine that is its source for life and growth. A branch has no life when it is cut off from the vine. Neither do we! Y'shua wants us to bear good fruit, but we can only do that if we remain close in our daily connection to Him. What kind of fruit does He want us to bear? Go back to Galatians 5:22 to find out!

EXPLORING SCRIPTURE

Look at the tree of life below. Look up the Scriptures and write a word or phrase beneath them to help you remember what the Scripture says you should do, or why it says you should do it, or what God will do for you because you are depending on Him. For example, in John 15, Y'shua tells us how He is the vine and we are the branches. John 15:4 tells us that a branch cannot bear fruit without the vine, so you could put the word "fruit" beneath the Scripture reference.

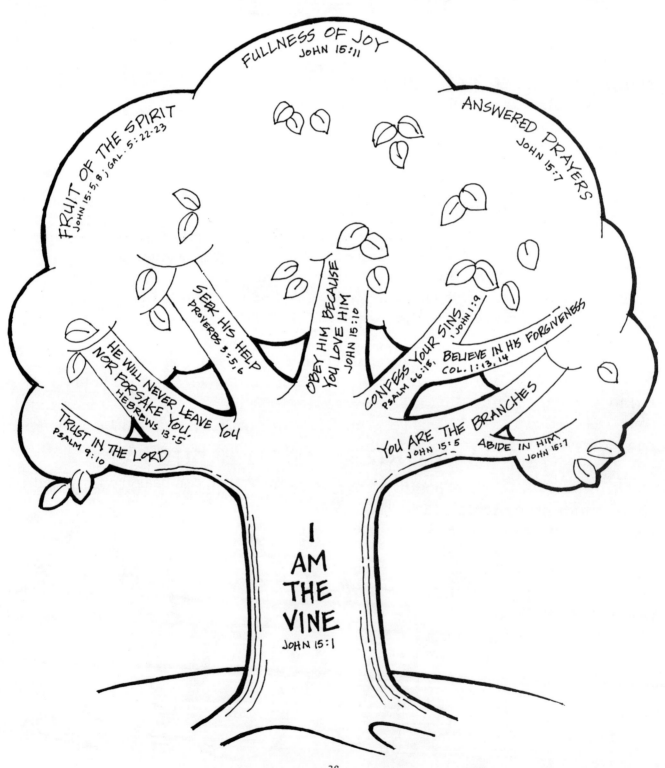

FULLNESS OF JOY
JOHN 15:11

FRUIT OF THE SPIRIT
JOHN 15:5,8; GAL. 5:22-23

ANSWERED PRAYERS
JOHN 15:7

SEEK HIS HELP
PROVERBS 3:5,6

OBEY HIM BECAUSE YOU LOVE HIM
JOHN 15:10

CONFESS YOUR SINS
1 JOHN 1:9
PSALM 66:18; BELIEVE IN HIS FORGIVENESS
COL. 1:13,14

HE WILL NEVER LEAVE YOU NOR FORSAKE YOU.
HEBREWS 13:5

TRUST IN THE LORD
PSALM 9:10

YOU ARE THE BRANCHES
JOHN 15:5

ABIDE IN HIM
JOHN 15:7

I AM THE VINE
JOHN 15:1

CELEBRATION IDEAS

• Make a Tu B' Shevat Planter!

What you need:
- clay flowerpot
- water-soluble acrylic paints—white for the base coat and your favorite colors
- Jewish stencils, sponges cut into small pieces for sponge painting
- paintbrushes
- "Mod Podge" or other shiny craft glaze
- Parsley seeds, potting soil or dirt, and garden tools

What you do:
- Paint your clay flowerpot with a base coat of white acrylic paint and let it dry.
- Plan your flowerpot design on paper.
- Paint or stencil Jewish symbols on your flowerpot using stencils, sponge shapes, or free-hand. Let your work dry.
- Cover your pot with "Mod Podge" to protect the finish. Let it dry.
- Add potting soil or dirt to the pot.
- Plant your parsley seeds and tend them following the package directions.
- Use your parsley at your family Passover Seder!

• Sing your favorite songs about trees to celebrate the holiday, like "Trees of the Field" and "Etz Chaim."

• Have a Tu B' Shevat "seder" where you enjoy different types of fruit and juice and read special Scripture portions about trees.

A VERSE TO MEMORIZE FOR TU B' SHEVAT

John 15:4 "Abide in me, and I will abide in you. No branch can bear fruit by itself; it must abide in the vine. Neither can you bear fruit unless you abide in me."

COLOR YOUR OWN HOLIDAY PICTURE

PURIM

A BIT OF BACKGROUND

A beautiful and courageous queen. An evil villain who wanted people to worship him. An honest man who loved God and did what was right regardless of the consequences! The holiday of Purim has captured the hearts of our people, not just because it's based upon a great story, but because that great story happens to be true!

Esther was a real-life Cinderella; an everyday girl who ended up marrying a king. Evil Haman (Boo!) was a powerful big shot who wanted to destroy the Jewish people, all because Mordecai would not bow down to him. Somebody had to tell King Ahasuerus about Haman's evil plot. Even though Esther was the queen, she knew she would be risking her life by going before the king without a special invitation. Mordecai told her, "Esther, God put you here on purpose—for such a time as this!" So Esther entrusted her life to God, and risked her life to save our people. God gave her favor in the king's eyes so that instead of having her executed for coming without an invitation, he was willing to give her whatever she asked.

Through their faith in the One True God, Esther and Mordecai found the courage to be part of God's rescue team. And Haman, who hated the Jews, God's people, ended up being put to death on the very gallows he had built to hang Mordecai!

God protected us back then and He has continued to preserve us—despite the plots of many enemies through the centuries. "Indeed, He who watches over Israel will neither slumber nor sleep!" (Psalm 121:4).

DIGGING DEEPER

Years later, Y'shua may have thought long and hard about Esther's brave example. Y'shua needed courage to carry out God's will to save our people, just as Esther had. But unlike Esther, Y'shua knew that He would have to die to obey God's plan for His life. Just think about the courage it took for Y'shua to face the cross! His courage to obey God did more than save our lives in this world—it made it possible for our souls to be saved so we could live with God forever and ever in the world to come. Now that is something to really celebrate!

The things that God asks you to do are not as scary as going in front of a king, much less dying on the cross! Still, God does ask us to do things that call for us to be brave. Have you ever made someone upset because you spoke up for what is right? Maybe at school all the kids are making fun of a particular boy or girl. They expect you to join in the jokes, to be cool. But you know that God wants you to be kind and to treat that boy or girl the way you want to be treated. What does it take for you to obey Him? What does it take for you to say "no" to many other things people want you to do, when you know those things are wrong?

It is not easy being brave when you aren't sure what will happen, and that is where trusting Y'shua comes in. Despite what you feel when you are afraid, Y'shua is there for you at that moment. He will give you the courage and strength to do the God-honoring thing. May you be like Esther, Mordecai, and Y'shua, with the courage to obey the will of your Father in heaven in big and little ways each day.

EXPLORING SCRIPTURE

Read: Esther 4:7-14

This passage tells how Mordecai sent a messenger to Esther, telling her of Haman's plot to destory the Jews and asking her to beg the king to help our people.

1. How long had it been since the king had asked to see Esther? Why was she afraid to go talk to the king?
2. What did Mordecai tell Esther would happen if she remained silent?
3. What did Esther do, and what did she ask all the Jews in the city to do for three days before she went to see the king?

Now read Joshua 1:9 and Hebrews 13:6

1. Why should we be strong and of good courage? Where can we go that God won't be with us?
2. Why should we not fear? Who is our helper?
3. Can you think of places and situations where it would help you to remember these verses?

OUR TRADITIONS

On Purim, Jewish children dress up in costumes and masks to play the parts of Esther, Mordecai, King Ahasuerus, and even Haman (Boo!) as we tell the story of Purim through drama and song. It's called a Purim Spiel or

Purim pageant. We eat hamantaschen— pastries filled with poppy seeds. Some say these three-cornered treats are shaped like Haman's hat or Haman's ears. Others think they resemble Haman's money bag!

We also read the whole book of Esther, known as the *Megillat* Esther. (A *megillah* is a scroll, and the Bible was orginally written on scrolls.) It takes a long time to read the entire story—so now you know what the phrase "the whole megillah" means! As we listen to the story, whenever we hear Haman's name, we boo loudly, stamp our feet and make lots of noise with *groggers* (holiday noisemakers) to drown his name out! And we cheer wildly whenever Esther and Mordecai are mentioned. That's probably why it takes us so long to read the story—we make a big megillah out of reading the whole megillah!

When God delivered us on that first Purim, Mordecai sent letters to Jewish people near and far telling them to celebrate by feasting, sending presents, and giving gifts to the poor. Today, Jewish people make and send Shalach Manot baskets of food and other goodies as a way to give gifts.

CELEBRATION IDEAS
• Have a Purim family outreach!
Read the story of Esther from your favorite Bible story book or from your Bible. Use this plan to help create your own special Purim Spiel (play). Invite your Jewish friends, relatives and neighbors and share the story of God's faithfulness to preserve our people. Take the opportunity to give a clear witness of Y'shua's love.

What you need:
Pray...about everything! Pray about who to invite, where and when to have your play, and for the script if you are writing one. Pray for God to give your loved ones open hearts and minds about who Y'shua really is.

Invitations. . . make your own invitations, writing the words on decorative scrolls made of colored paper. Hand-deliver the scrolls to those who live close enough to you and mail the rest.

Purchase. . . the paper cups, plates, and napkins, hamantaschen ingredients, drinks, party decorations, and any costume accessories you need for the play.

Prop box. . . collect all the props and costumes you'll need for the characters in your play.

Scripts. . .
The Easy Way... copy the story of Esther from a children's Bible and use it to narrate your play while the actors pantomime what the narrator is saying.

A bit more work. . . use the same basic story, but write some speaking parts for your characters.

For the very ambitious. . . use your writing skills to create your own original play, based on the Scriptures.

Decide. . . who will play what parts and how to share Y'shua with your guests. Perhaps you could have a character say that God preserved us for a purpose—to know Him and the Messiah He's sent, and then say something about Y'shua and how He also did a brave thing to save His people.

Make Hamantaschen. . . use your favorite family recipe, or use the recipe in the *Jews for Jesus Family Cookbook.*

What to do. . . the day of the Spiel:
   - Greet your guests
   - Lights, camera, Purim action!
   - Celebrate with refreshments
   - Talk to your friends and relatives—tell them you are glad they came
   - Praise God for this opportunity to share about Y'shua

• **Shalach Manot baskets for Purim**
Make Shalach-manot baskets for people you love or take baskets to a home for the elderly to brighten their holiday.

What you need:
   - small baskets
   - a variety of ribbon
   - cardboard
   - napkins with Jewish symbols or colors
   - hamantaschen and other holiday treats

What you do:
   - weave ribbon through the holes in the basket to decorate
   - cut cardboard to fit the bottom of the basket
   - lay your decorative napkin in the basket
   - fill your basket with treats and deliver!

A VERSE TO MEMORIZE FOR PURIM
Joshua 1:9 "Have I not commanded you? Be strong and of good courage; do not be afraid, nor be dismayed, for the LORD your God is with you wherever you go."

PASSOVER

A BIT OF BACKGROUND

Pesach (Hebrew for Passover) tells the remarkable story of God's power in action and how He sets His people free so we can love and serve Him. You can read about Passover in Exodus 12, and you can also read about it in the Haggadah on your seder table. With trembling hearts, our people carried out God's specific instructions to Moses. The Passover lamb of long ago brought us redemption from slavery as its blood was painted on the doorposts of Jewish homes in obedience to God. That blood was a sign that told the angel of death to pass over the firstborn children of Israel on that solemn night in Egypt. The songs we sing, the stories we tell, even the traditional foods we eat help us to understand God's love for His people, and how He provided an escape from slavery and from death.

DIGGING DEEPER

Passover is actually the tale of two different lambs, from different times in Jewish history. The blood of the first Passover lambs in Egypt told the plague of death, "Leave the Jewish people alone! These people are God's people!" Many years later, God sent another lamb, Y'shua, to die for the sins of the whole world. The story of the first lamb and our redemption from Egypt helps us recognize Y'shua, the second Lamb, and how His death and resurrection made it possible for us to be free from sin and death. When we receive Y'shua as our Messiah and Lord, the blood of the Lamb of God seals the doorposts of our hearts, showing that we are His people. If we believe in the sacrifice of God's Lamb, we have a second kind of Passover— a spiritual one, where we pass from spiritual death (separation from God caused by our sin) into eternal life and a forever relationship with our loving God.

Remembering great miracles helps us trust God. As we remember God's power in bringing our people out of Egypt, it will give us courage to rely on Him to bring us out of the troubles we may face today.

Y'shua had a very special Passover with His disciples just before He died on the cross. During the seder He used the symbols of the Passover to point to Himself. He knew that He was about to suffer and die, just like the lamb at the first Passover. He told His disciples they should remember Him whenever they ate the broken matza and drank the fruit of the vine. Most churches today have special times to do this. They might call it communion or the Lord's supper. Maybe your congregation has another name for it. It would be a very sad time as we think about Y'shua's broken body and His blood, except for one thing. Y'shua told us that He would one day drink the fruit of the vine in the Kingdom of God. . . . He was saying that His death is not the end of the story—and we know that is true because He rose from the dead!

EXPLORING SCRIPTURE

Read: Isaiah 53:5-8

1. Whose transgression (sin) does verse 5 and 8 say this person dies for?
2. What animal is this person compared to?
3. Who do you think this passage is talking about?

Now read: Mark 14:22-25, which tells about the special Passover Y'shua had with His disciples.

1. What did Y'shua say about the piece of bread (matza)?
2. What did He say about the cup?
3. When did He say He would drink again from the cup? How could He say He was going to drink it again if He knew He was about to die on the cross?

OUR TRADITIONS

There are lots and lots of Passover traditions; way too many to mention here, but the Passover Haggadah tells about them. A favorite holiday tradition is the *afikomen* search. The word *afikomen* means, "that which comes after." During Passover, the middle piece of matza from the matza tosh is removed and broken. Half goes back into the matza

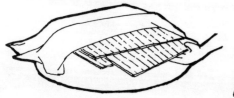
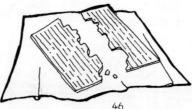
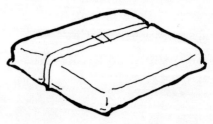

tosh, but the other half gets wrapped in a special cloth or a napkin. It's called the afikomen, and it gets hidden away somewhere, buried beneath something. Searching for the afikomen is a tradition that Jewish children have enjoyed for years! Until they find it, we can't complete the seder. The afikomen is the last thing we eat at the seder and it tells a story about Y'shua that many of our Jewish people don't know. Look at the pictures and see what they show you!

CELEBRATION IDEAS

• Search out the leaven

Help your parents prepare for Passover by taking part in a family chomaytz (leaven) hunt. Search every corner of your home. As you get rid of the leaven, think about getting rid of sin in your life. You can use this ceremony in the *Haggadah* to help you dedicate your heart to following Y'shua in a clean, fresh way. Discuss with your family how you can break out of sinful habits. Pray that God will help you live a holy life in Y'shua.

• Add something to the tradition of the afikomen and the

third cup (the cup of Redemption) that we drink after eating it. Does the tradition of the afikomen remind you of anything that happened to Y'shua? Y'shua died on the cross, was wrapped in linen and buried in a tomb for a time. But just like the afikomen is brought back, God brought Y'shua back to life! We aren't really sure how this custom became a part of the Haggadah. Some people think that Y'shua's first disciples added this to the seder after He went to heaven to help them remember what happened to Him. Anyway, the afikomen can help us remember Him when we celebrate Passover. There are traditional blessings that we say when we eat the bread and drink the wine, but as believers in Y'shua, your family can add your own prayers to them, thanking Y'shua for allowing His body to be broken and His blood to be shed for us.

• Paint a plate for Passover!

What you need

- a Hagaddah with pictures of the seder plate items
- a large, clear glass plate
- enamel paint suitable for glass (a good brand is "Apple Barrel Gloss Paint" by Spouncer)

- medium, thin, and fine paintbrushes
- oven
- container of water
- paper towels
- newspaper to protect work space

What you do:
- Plan your design with pencil on a piece of paper before you paint. Decide if you want to make a traditional seder plate, or a regular plate with Passover designs.
- Paint the plate (paint on the opposite side of the plate if it will be used for food).
- Use Jewish symbols, pictures, or Bible verses.
- Allow plate to dry at least 48 hours.
- Place in oven. Heat oven to 325 degrees. Bake for 15 minutes.
- Turn oven off and keep plate inside till the oven is cold.
- Use on your seder table!

• Charoset Around The Jewish World

No matter where it's from, *charoset* is sweet! But it represents the mortar used by our people to build the great storage cities for Pharaoh—so why do we make it taste so good? The rabbis said "even the bitterest of our labors grew sweet when we knew that our redemption drew near." How much more can we experience the sweetness of redemption now that we know Y'shua!

Because our Jewish people have lived in many different places, there are probably as many recipes for *charoset* as there are countries in which we've wandered! Try making this unusual *charoset* recipe from Italy and taste for yourself how Passover celebrations differ depending on where Jewish people live.

Charoset from Italy (no spaghetti, please!)
- 2 apples, finely chopped
- 6 dates, finely chopped
- 1 hard-boiled egg, finely chopped
- 1/2 cup almonds, finely chopped
- 6 walnuts, finely chopped
- 1/4 cup raisins, finely chopped
- matzo meal as needed
- 1 teaspoon of lemon juice

Combine the ingredients, adding enough matzo meal to keep the mixture together.

A VERSE TO MEMORIZE FOR PASSOVER

John 5:24 "Truly, truly, I say to you, he who hears My word and believes on Him who sent Me has everlasting life and shall not come into condemnation, but has passed from death to life."

Y'SHUA'S RESURRECTION DAY

A BIT OF BACKGROUND

When Y'shua died on the cross, the whole city of Jerusalem was in an uproar. His disciples were afraid they might be punished for being His friends. Yet some who had heard Him say that He would rise from the dead wondered what would happen next. Certain leaders feared that the disciples might try to steal Y'shua's body to make it look like He had risen from the dead. So they sealed His tomb with a huge stone, a boulder so heavy that many strong men had to put it in place. Then the special seal of the Roman government was placed on it and Roman guards were ordered to watch the tomb. If anyone tried to move the stone, the Roman seal would be broken. The guards would be executed for failing to do their job. The weight of the stone, the Roman guards, the seal and the disciples' fear made one thing certain: Y'shua's body would stay put.

And yet, three days after Y'shua died on the cross, the women who came to visit the tomb saw an amazing sight. The stone that covered the mouth of the tomb had been rolled back! Y'shua's body was gone, but the grave clothes were still there. (The burial cloth that Y'shua was wound in had a sticky paste of spices holding it in place, according to Jewish custom.) All that the women saw where His body had been was an empty shell! God had raised Y'shua from the dead just as Y'shua had promised. There is no other explanation for the empty tomb!

DIGGING DEEPER

When Y'shua rose from the dead, it proved something very important: He had lived a perfect life and did not deserve any punishment for sin. You see, if Y'shua had deserved the same punishment we do for sin, He could not have died to take our place. Y'shua's resurrection means that He truly did die for our sins. But it also points to something wonderful that will one day happen to all of us who believe in Him.

You see, following Passover, there is a Jewish holiday called "the Feast of Firstfruits." God commanded our people to make "firstfruit offerings" several times during the year. In Bible times, firstfruits meant the very beginning of the harvest. Different crops were harvested at different times of the year. God wanted our people to give Him the firstfruit that we harvested as a reminder that all our blessings and all our crops came from Him. By offering Him the firstfruits, we were telling God, "You have a right to everything we have, since everything we have (including ourselves!) belongs to You." But we were also saying something else to God. We were saying, "We give You the first part of our harvest because we trust You and we know You will send more crops to meet our needs."

Y'shua came back to life on the Feast of Firstfruits! Just like the firstfruits from the crops were a way of saying "there will be more of a harvest to come," Y'shua's resurrection on the Feast of Firstfruits was God's way of saying, "Y'shua is the first of many who will conquer death."

There are two kinds of death, and both of them have to do with separation. The worst kind is spiritual death. The Bible tells us that sin separates us from God and being separated from Him is spiritual death. But when God forgives our sin (which He does when we accept that Y'shua died for us and rose again), we become spiritually alive! The other kind of death is physical. When we die, our souls are separated from our bodies. If we are spiritually alive, we don't have to worry about the fact that our bodies will die some day, because our souls will go to be with God forever and ever. But the Bible says that one day God is going to give brand new bodies to all the believers in Y'shua. Y'shua was the first one to get a "resurrection" body.

EXPLORING SCRIPTURE

Read John 2:19-22

1. What did the Temple symbolize?
2. How many days did Y'shua say it would take to raise it up?
3. Can you guess why it is important that Y'shua predicted what would happen?

Read John 20:19

1. The disciples had locked the doors; how do you think Y'shua came to be standing in their midst?
2. Do you think His body was exactly the same as it was before He rose from the dead?

Read 1 Corinthians 15:6

1. How many people does the apostle Paul say that Y'shua appeared to after He rose from the dead?
2. Can you guess why it is important that so many people saw Him?

Read 1 Corinthians 15:20

1. When a person falls asleep, they can wake up. Why do you think this verse describes people who are dead as "those who have fallen asleep?"

2. What does it mean when it says Y'shua is the firstfruits? Can you have firstfruits without there being more "fruit" to come? If Jesus is the firstfruits, who are the rest of the "fruits?"

OUR TRADITIONS

As with Y'shua's birthday, most of our Jewish people have no traditions to celebrate Y'shua's resurrection because they don't yet believe that He rose from the dead. But many religious Jewish people recite a statement called "The 13 Principles of the Faith" every day. Each "principle of faith" is a teaching that all Jewish people are supposed to believe. The last of those principles of faith says, "I believe with perfect faith that there will be a revival of the dead at the time when it shall please the Creator, blessed be His Name, and exalted be His fame for ever and ever. For thy salvation I hope, O Lord!" So even though the majority of our Jewish people do not believe that Jesus rose from the dead, the Jewish religion teaches that there will be a resurrection.

CELEBRATION IDEAS

- **This combination cookie recipe/Bible study** tells the story of Y'shua's death and resurrection. Do the first part before bedtime. As you follow the instructions, rejoice in what our Messiah has done!

What you need:
- 1 cup whole peanuts
- 1 teaspoon vinegar
- 1 cup sugar
- masking tape
- Bible
- 3 egg whites
- pinch of salt
- wooden spoon
- large zip-lock bag

What you do:
- Preheat the oven to 300 degrees.
- Place peanuts in the zip lock bag. Pound them into small pieces with a wooden spoon.

Read John 19:1-2 and think about how Y'shua was arrested and beaten by Roman soldiers.

- Smell the vinegar, then put one teaspoon of it into a mixing bowl.

Read John 19:28-30 and think about how Y'shua was given vinegar to drink when He was on the cross.

- Add the egg whites to the vinegar.

Read John 3:14-16. Did you know that in Jewish tradition, eggs represent life? Y'shua gives us eternal life that no one can ever take away from us!

- Sprinkle a few grains of salt into your hand and taste them. Now wash your hands and put a little pinch of salt into the bowl.

Read Luke 23:27 and think about how Y'shua's friends cried salty tears because He had to suffer on the cross.

- Add one cup of sugar to the bowl.

Read Romans 5:8 and think how the sweetest part of this true story is that Y'shua died because He loves us and wants to give us eternal life.

- Beat the mixture with a mixer at high speed for 12-15 minutes, until stiff peaks are formed.

Read Isaiah 1:18 and 1 John 1:9 and let the white color remind you of purity, and cleansing. We become clean when we confess our sins to Y'shua. and receive His forgiveness personally. When we do this for the first time, we become followers of Y'shua and children of God.

- Fold in the broken nuts. Drop teaspoons of mixture onto a wax paper-covered cookie sheet.

Read Matthew 27:57-60. Don't these cookie mounds look like rocks? Think about the huge rock that covered the doorway of the tomb where they placed Y'shua's body.

- Put the cookie sheet into the oven, close the door and turn the oven OFF. Seal the door shut with masking tape so no one can open it.

Read Matthew 27:62-66 and think about how Y'shua's tomb was sealed with the Roman seal, and how guards were posted so no one could enter.

- Don't read any further until morning! It's time to go to sleep now, and wait to see what will happen.

- In the morning, take the tape off the door and open the oven. Look at the cracked surface of the cookies. Take a bite. The cookies are hollow, empty inside.

Read Luke 24:1-12 and rejoice! On the third day, Y'shua's tomb was empty! He rose from the dead! Hallelujah!

A VERSE TO MEMORIZE FOR Y'SHUA'S RESURRECTION

1 Corinthians 15:20 "But now Messiah is risen from the dead, and has become the firstfruits of those who have fallen asleep."

SHAVUOT

A BIT OF BACKGROUND

Shavuot gets its name from the Hebrew word for "weeks," because it is celebrated seven weeks after Passover. Another name for Shavuot is "Pentecost." "Pente" is the Greek word for 50 and we celebrate Shavuot exactly 50 days after Passover! This two-day spring holiday has a double meaning.

First, it is a "spring harvest" celebration. In Bible times, our holiday celebrations were closely tied in with the cycle of planting and reaping. That was God's idea, to help us understand that we depend on Him for everything. He doesn't like us to take His blessings for granted. In fact, between Passover and Shavuot, God commanded our people to count out measures of grain called an "omer." A holiday that you won't see in the Bible, but one that religious Jewish people observe today is called "Lag b'Omer" which has to do with counting the omer. Instead of counting out measures of grain, people usually just count the days between Passover and Shavuot.

Anyway, when our ancestors were farmers in Israel, there was great rejoicing as they gathered in the wheat crops during Shavuot.

The second meaning of Shavuot has to do with a Jewish tradition that says God gave us the Ten Commandments on Mount Sinai seven weeks after Passover. Receiving those commandments helped make our ancestors into a community. We all understood how God wanted us to behave and we were supposed to help each other to obey His ways.

Later, God gave other commands to help us know how to behave. God wanted people to treat one another kindly, and that comes through in the way He commanded us to celebrate Shavuot (see Leviticus 23:15-22). God told our people that when we gathered in our crops, we were not to harvest every bit of grain from the field. We were to leave some for strangers and for people who could not afford to buy food. The work of picking up the grain that was left behind was called "gleaning."

God also commanded us to bake two special loaves of bread with flour made from the first and the best of our newly harvested grain. These loaves of bread had to be perfect because we were going to offer them to God. Like the "firstfruits" a few days after Passover, this was another firstfruit celebration to show God that we trusted Him to continue providing for us.

On Shavuot, Jewish people made a special trip called a pilgrimage to Jerusalem, where they presented those special firstfruit offerings, called *bikkurim,* in the Temple. No one was allowed to work on Shavuot. It was to be a happy time of joyous music, dancing and hearts filled with thanks to God for His goodness.

DIGGING DEEPER

In celebrating Shavuot, we also celebrate the end of Passover. Remember how God set our ancestors free from slavery? What were we set free to do? God answered that question when He gave us the Ten Commandments. Now we knew what God expected of us—to live in right relationship with Him and with each other. But even though we knew what to do, we didn't have the power within us to obey Him all the time.

The prophet Jeremiah told of a wonderful promise God made. He said that one day the power to obey God would come from within us because of a miracle He would create in our hearts. God said He would write on our hearts those things He wants us to do! He didn't mean writing with an actual pen, but that we would be able to obey Him because of something He would do inside of us.

Before Y'shua went to heaven, He told His disciples to wait in Jerusalem for a gift. That gift was the Holy Spirit, who fulfilled the promise that God made through the prophet Jeremiah! Just like the Ten Commandments were given to the Jewish people on Shavuot, the Holy Spirit came upon Y'shua's first disciples during Shavuot, giving them power to live out God's truth daily. If you know Y'shua personally, you have His Spirit in your heart, too! He will give you power to live for Him. Just ask!

EXPLORING SCRIPTURE

Read: Jeremiah 31:31-33

"'Behold, the days are coming, says the LORD, when I will make a new covenant with the house of Israel and with the house of Judah—not according to the covenant that I made with their fathers in the day that I took them by the hand to lead them out of the land of Egypt, because of my covenant which they broke, though I was a husband to them,' says the LORD. 'But this is the covenant that I will make with the house of Israel after those days,' says the LORD: 'I will put My law in their minds, and write it on their hearts; and I will be their God, and they shall be My people.'" (Jeremiah 31:31-33).

1. A covenant is an agreement that has certain promises attached to it. What kind of covenant does God say He will make with the house of Israel?
2. What happened to the old covenant that God made with our ancestors when He led them out of Egypt?
3. Where does God say He will put His law?

Read: John 14:16-17
1. How long will the helper, whom Jesus promised, stay with us?
2. Who do you think the Spirit of truth is?

Now read: Romans 8:16, 26
1. Who is "the Spirit himself?"
2. Whose children does that Spirit say we are?

OUR TRADITIONS

We celebrate Shavuot by decorating our place of worship with fresh fruits, remembering the firstfruits once brought to the Temple. We also decorate our homes with leafy branches, fruit and wildflowers. Everyone gathers the night before Shavuot for an all-night Torah study session called *"tikkun leil Shavuot."* If you can manage to stay awake till the morning service, you'll hear readings from the Ten Commandments and also from the book of Ruth, because the story of Ruth tells about something special that happened during a harvest festival. The story of Ruth is also important because it shows that people who are not Jewish can be part of our community if they love the God of Israel.

According to Jewish tradition, our people were too tired to cook when they returned home after receiving the Ten Commandments. Since there were no fast-food restaurants in Bible times, they probably prepared easy-to-fix foods like milk and cheese. We continue that tradition by eating dairy products on Shavuot.

CELEBRATION IDEAS
• **Have a Family Slumber Party!**
  - Try the Jewish tradition of staying up all night to study the Bible by using the following plan:
  - Read or act out the story of Ruth, and discuss God's plan to include the Gentiles in His family.
  - Watch Bible videos.
  - Listen to messianic music.

Bake and pray

Bake two loaves of bread, either from scratch or from store-bought dough. Let one loaf represent Jewish people, the other represent Gentiles. Write the names of people you care about, who still need to know Y'shua, on a plastic or paper tray. Place the loaves on the tray. Pray for these people who are so important to God.

Eat

Choose dairy foods like blintzes, kugel, or cheese souffle. Try creating a new recipe!

Decorate

Make a *bikkurim* basket with leafy vines and flowers for decoration, and add food to donate to the community food bank. Decorate your home for the holiday with fresh flowers and greenery.

Discuss

With your family, talk about what it means to give your best to God. Spend time brainstorming then write out a plan to help you give your best to God.

A VERSE TO MEMORIZE FOR SHAVUOT

Jeremiah 31:33 "'But this is the covenant that I will make with the house of Israel after those days,' says the LORD: 'I will put My law in their minds, and write it on their hearts; and I will be their God, and they shall be My people.'"

TISHA B' AV

A BIT OF BACKGROUND

Tisha b'Av is a sad time for our people because it marks the date when both the first and second Temples were destroyed.

King David's son, Solomon, built the first Temple. It was so very beautiful that it was considered one of the wonders of the ancient world. Unfortunately, Solomon's heart strayed from God. He married foreign wives who worshipped idols and many of his children turned to false gods. As our people continued in idolatry, God sent judgment through King Nebuchadnezzar of Babylon. His army destroyed the Temple in 586 B.C.E. on Tisha b'Av and his soldiers carried the Israelites off into captivity.

Years later, in 538 B.C.E., King Cyrus of Persia defeated Babylon and our people began to return to the land, just as God had promised they would. Zerubbabel was in charge of rebuilding the Temple. This was a very important job because without the Temple, there was no proper way to make a sacrifice, and without a sacrifice, how could our people receive God's forgiveness?

DIGGING DEEPER

Y'shua was born during the time when the Roman Empire ruled practically the whole world. They treated our people harshly and this created a special longing for the Messiah. We wanted Him to come and get rid of the Romans!

When Y'shua announced the coming of God's kingdom, the Roman officials and Jewish leaders became very nervous. Who was this carpenter from Galilee? What was He going to do? Some people thought He would raise an army and try to overthrow the government, which could make a lot of trouble for the Jewish people. But Y'shua had other plans. He came to overcome the power of sin and death. He did that when He died for our sins and rose from the dead.

Soon after Y'shua went back to heaven, a terrible thing happened. On Tisha b'Av in 70 C.E., Roman soldiers burned the second Temple and destroyed Jerusalem. Our people were devastated at the terrible loss of life and the loss of our Temple. Those who didn't understand about Y'shua's sacrifice were the saddest of all. How could they have their sin covered now? What would they do without the Temple?

Eventually, Jewish leaders met to discuss the problem. They did their best to come up with something that might work as an atonement for sins. They agreed that God would forgive us if we did three things instead of animal sacrifice: *tzedakah* (good works), *t'shuvah* (repentance), and *tefillah* (prayer). All of these things are good and right to do but they don't work as a substitute for God's way of atonement, which is Y'shua and His sacrifice. People can agree on things that sound good to us but that doesn't make those things true. Something is true if it agrees with God's Word.

EXPLORING SCRIPTURE

King David wrote many wonderful Psalms, including Psalm 69. In verse nine, he wrote: " . . . zeal for Your house has eaten me up, and the reproaches of those who reproach You have fallen on me." King David was talking to God, so "your house" means God's house. David got terribly upset when people reproached (blamed or found fault with) God. David had a burning desire for people to love and respect God the way that he did, the way they should. Y'shua, the Messiah, a descendant of David, felt the same way!

Read: John 2:13-22

1. What did Y'shua find in the Temple?

2. What did He make, and what did He do with what He made?

3. What was Y'shua referring to when He said, "My Father's house"?

4. What did the disciples remember when they heard Y'shua talk about His Father's house?

5. When you go to worship with your congregation, does it matter what people around you are doing and saying? How would you feel if people sitting near you acted like they were not interested in worshipping the Lord?

6. When Y'shua spoke about the Temple being destroyed and raised in three days, was He talking about a building? What was He talking about? Did it happen?

OUR TRADITIONS

Our people fast from sunset to sunset on Tisha b'Av and read the book of Lamentations. It was written by Jeremiah whose heart was broken by the destruction of Jerusalem and the first Temple. Years later, Y'shua would weep over Jerusalem just as Jeremiah did. He still grieves over our people who've rejected His sacrifice for their sin.

CELEBRATION IDEAS

We don't celebrate Tisha b'Av so much as we remember. It's right to feel sad that so many of our people died when the Temple was destroyed. And we feel sad that so many of our people do not understand that Y'shua is our once and for all sacrifice. But even while we are sad, we can still be glad that we know Y'shua and we can ask God to help us show others that He is true.

- **Thank God** for preserving our Jewish people through many dark times.

- **Pray and fast** as we ask God to help our people believe in Y'shua as the Messiah and accept His offering for our sins and to protect our people in the land of Israel and around the world.

- **Praise God** for giving us Y'shua so we can be forgiven.

A VERSE TO MEMORIZE FOR TISHA B'AV

Revelation 21:22 "I did not see a temple in the city, because the Lord God Almighty and the Lamb are its temple."

COLOR YOUR OWN HOLIDAY PICTURE

YOM HA ATZMA'UT—
HAPPY BIRTHDAY ISRAEL!

A BIT OF BACKGROUND

Once the Romans took over the Land of Israel, our people had no claim to it for nearly 2,000 years. Even after the Roman Empire fell, other nations came and claimed the land as their own. But on May 14, 1948, the United Nations voted to support the declaration of Israel as an independent nation where Jewish people could live on their own again! The modern state of Israel was born in one day and since then, Jewish people from over 70 countries have made *aliyah* (moved to Israel). God did an amazing thing in using other countries and circumstances to give us back our Land. We mourn over the destruction of the Temple and our exile on Tisha b'Av but then we get to celebrate Yom Ha Atzma'ut (Israel's Indepence Day) on the fifth of Iyar. Many people see Israel's independence as a modern miracle but if you know the Scriptures, this miracle should come as no surprise. God did just as He promised!

DIGGING DEEPER

When God makes a promise to His people, He means it and we can depend on Him to keep His word. People may fail us but God never will! Sometimes we can see His promises come true right away, and sometimes we have to wait for what seems like a very long time. But even while we wait, God wants us to trust Him and believe His promises. We can know what He has promised by reading His Word. "And we have the word of the prophets made more certain, and you will do well to pay attention to it, as to a light shining in a dark place, until the day dawns and the morning star rises in your hearts" (2 Peter 1:19).

Yom Ha Atzma'ut is a special celebration because God promised to bring our people back to the Land of Israel, and He did! He did not forget us or His covenant with Abraham. But there is another promise that we are still waiting for God to keep.

You see, today in the land of Israel, most people are secular Jews, living lives apart from God. The prophet Zechariah said that one day the whole world will recognize Y'shua, who will return to *Eretz* Israel. People from every country will come to Jerusalem. Why? To worship the Lord and celebrate the festival of Sukkot with us! (Zechariah 14:16-19).

EXPLORING SCRIPTURE

God's Promise
Read: Genesis 12:1-3 and Genesis 13:14-17

God promised Abraham land, nationhood and blessing.

1. Who did God say He would bless and who did He say He would curse?
2. Who did God say He was giving the land to, besides Abraham? What does that mean?
3. For how long did God say He was giving the Land to Abraham?

Now read: Deuteronomy 30:4-6

When we disobeyed God, we had to leave the Promised Land for awhile. God said that one day our people would return to the place He gave us—and He would help us all to love and obey Him. We pray that this Scripture will soon be fulfilled in the lives of Jewish people all over the world as they recognize Y'shua, their true King!

1. Where did God say He would gather our Jewish people from?
2. Where did God say He would bring us?
3. God said we would love Him with all of our _____, and with all of our _____. What do you think that means?

OUR TRADITIONS

Israel celebrates Yom Ha'Atzma'ut with parties and parades. Our people sing, dance and enjoy bonfires. The Israeli Air Force puts on a spectacular show to honor the country's birthday. Jewish people living in other lands also celebrate. Even those of us who don't live in Israel are happy that our people have their own land.

CELEBRATION IDEAS

• **Make a Birthday Party for Israel!**

Invitations: Make invitations in blue and white—the color of Israel's flag.

Food: Prepare an Israeli meal using recipes from your favorite Jewish cookbook. Then have a birthday cake for dessert!

Activities:

Create a pretend "tell" (archaeological site) using sand and find "buried" items from past centuries. Add treasures of gelt, glass jewels, or shekels for children to keep.

What you need:

- a large sandbox or area in your backyard you can cover with clean sand
- a bag of small glass "jewels" from the craft store
- "ancient artifacts" you find or create: small clay pots or jars, scrolls made of paper attached to small dowels, toy figurines, coins from Israel, cast-off costume jewelry, discarded candle holders, etc., as well as some cast-off items from modern times that children might enjoy
- zip-lock bags and a small toy shovel for each "archeologist" who will work at the "tell" making discoveries

What you do:

Before your celebration, prepare the "tell" by placing some of the artifacts down on a small layer of sand either in a sandbox or in a designated area of your backyard. This first layer will be the oldest layer of your "tell." Make sure there is a good amount of space between the objects in each layer. Cover it evenly and carefully with sand so nothing shows through. Put down the next layer of artifacts that are a bit more modern and cover with sand. Keep adding layers, ending with a top layer of sand. Give each person a small toy shovel and a zip-lock bag to store his or her discoveries.

Try some Israeli folk dances.

End the celebration Israeli-style—with a kumsitz! Sit by the fire and sing Israeli folk songs. Include "Hatikvah" and "Hinei Mah Tov"!

• Pray for the Peace of Jerusalem

Using the word SHALOM make an acrostic guide to help you pray for our people. (For example, the S could remind you to pray for the salvation of our people, the H that our people would know they can call upon God for help, etc.)

A VERSE TO MEMORIZE FOR YOM HA ATZMA'UT

Isaiah 66:8 "Who has ever heard of such a thing? Who has ever seen such things? Can a country be born in a day or a nation be brought forth in a moment? Yet no sooner is Zion in labor than she gives birth to her children."

COLOR YOUR OWN HOLIDAY PICTURE

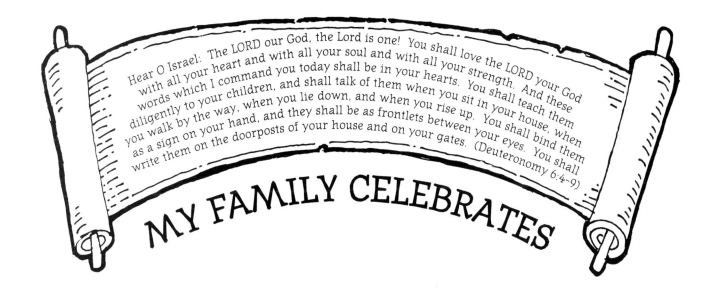

Hear O Israel: The LORD our God, the Lord is one! You shall love the LORD your God with all your heart and with all your soul and with all your strength. And these words which I command you today shall be in your hearts. You shall teach them diligently to your children, and shall talk of them when you sit in your house, when you walk by the way, when you lie down, and when you rise up. You shall bind them as a sign on your hand, and they shall be as frontlets between your eyes. You shall write them on the doorposts of your house and on your gates. (Deuteronomy 6:4-9)

MY FAMILY CELEBRATES

INSTRUCTIONS:

Use the following page as a sample of questions to answer after each holiday celebration. You might need more than one piece of paper to answer the questions. That's OK. Take as much space as you need to record what you did and what you think. Use loose-leaf paper or get a three-hole punch so you can keep your answers for your family holiday notebook. Add photographs and/or drawings of your celebration. Save copies of invitations or holiday artwork that you created. Keep scripts of holiday plays you wrote and acted out. When the year is over, look through your journal to help you remember the wonderful things you did together to celebrate Y'shua through the year. See how you've grown in understanding God's love for you, and in passing that love on to others!

A note about spiritual milestones: You might want to make spiritual milestone pages that go between the holidays since some of the big things in your life might happen on ordinary days, not holidays. Think about the things that you can write to remind yourself of your walk with God and His faithfulness in your life. It's good to see these things as treasures to keep in your heart. Sometimes when you don't feel like God is very real in your life, it helps to look back and remember what He did for you and your family. Remembering helps you feel close to God again. Some milestones to record are: your decision to follow Y'shua, obeying Y'shua in baptism or messianic mikvah, Bar or Bat mitzvah, reading the four questions at Passover for the first time, saying the Shabbat blessings for the first time, sharing your faith in Y'shua for the first time . . . and many other things that you can think of on your own!

MY FAMILY CELEBRATES!

Year: _____

We remembered God by celebrating _____ on the
(holiday)

_____ , the _____ .
(Jewish calendar date)   (solar calendar date)

This is what we discovered about Y'shua and his love: _____

_____

_____

_____

Our family memorized this Scripture verse (write out the whole verse!):

_____

_____

_____

Our favorite activity was: _____

_____

_____

_____

Something funny that happened was . . . _____

_____

_____

_____

People we celebrated with were . . . _____

_____

_____

_____

_____

_____

_____

A spiritual milestone in _____'s life was _____ .
                   (name)

Next year I want to celebrate by . . .

_____

_____

_____

_____

_____

_____

_____

_____

_____

_____

_____

_____

_____

_____

_____

_____

_____

RESOURCE LIST

- *A Family Guide to the Biblical Holidays with Activities for all Ages* by Robin Scarlata & Linda Pierce, Family Christian Press, 487 Myatt Drive, Madison TN 37115, (615) 860-3000.

  This wonderful resource is filled with good, practical ideas for celebrating the biblical holidays. It was written specifically for homeschoolers but is helpful for those not on the homeschool track as well.

- *Fun Excuses to Talk About God: 48 no fuss Family Devotions* by Joani Schultz, Group Publishing, PO Box 481, Loveland CO 80539-0481. Available from Purple Pomegranate Productions.

  This devotional guide for families lives up to its title: it is fun and not the least bit "stuffy."

- Making Scripture Stick: 52 Unforgettable Bible Verse Adventures for Children by Lisa Flinn & Barbara Younger, Group Publishing, PO Box 485, Loveland CO 80539-0485. Available from Purple Pomegranate Productions.

  Creative and memorable ways to get the Word of God into your kids' hearts.

- *Teaching the Bible Creatively, How to Awaken Your Kids to Scripture* by Bill McNabb & Steven Mabry, Youth Specialties, PO Box 668, Holmes PA 19043-9631, (800) 776-8008.

  This has many good ideas for making Scripture come alive for your children.

- *The Land & People Jesus Knew,* written & illustrated by J. Robert Teringo, Bethany House Publishers, Minneapolis MN 55438.

  The illustrations and text help children see the way people lived when Y'shua walked the earth.

- *The Jews for Jesus Family Cookbook* by Melissa Moskowitz, Purple Pomegranate Productions, (415) 864-3900.

  This cookbook is loaded with wonderful recipes and stories to help your family celebrate the joyful times and seasons of the year!

- *Yeladim for Y'shua,* a music tape produced by Jews for Jesus, Purple Pomegranate Productions, (415) 864-3900.

  Jewish children sing Y'shua's praises. "The B'racha Song" includes the Shabbat blessings and the Shehechiyanu Prayer in Hebrew. The "Aleph-Bet" song helps children of all ages learn the Hebrew alphabet. Songbook is included.

- *You Gotta Jump!* is another music tape produced by Jews for Jesus, Purple Pomegranate Productions, (415) 864-3900. It includes a wonderful Shabbat medley and other songs of hope and joy that your children will love.

- *Tu B'Shevat Seder for Jewish believers:* We've written one that we'll be glad to send. Write to: Youth Ministry Coordinator, Jews for Jesus, 60 Haight Street, San Francisco CA 94102.